ANDREA JAMES is a Yorta Yorta/Gunaikurnai woman and a graduate of the Victorian College of the Arts. She makes work that reflects her identity, sharing historical and contemporary stories of Aboriginal experiences within sharp contemporary theatrical language and form. Andrea is an experienced collaborator, playwright, producer and director. She was a recipient of British Council's Accelerate Program for Aboriginal Art Leaders in 2013 and was awarded an Arts NSW Aboriginal Arts Fellowship. She has produced for Carriageworks, Blacktown Arts Centre and Urban Theatre Projects. She was Artistic Director of Melbourne Workers Theatre 2001-2008 where she is best known for her play *Yanagai! Yanagai!* She co-wrote *Coranderrk* with Giordano Nanni for La Mama and Ilbijerri, *Bright World* with Elise Hearst for Arthur Productions, and wrote *Blacktown Angels* for *Home Country* for Urban Theatre Projects, *Bukal* for JUTE Theatre, and *Winyanboga Yurringa* for Moogahlin Performing Arts which was remounted at Belvoir in May 2019. Her works have shown throughout Australia, in the UK, Paris and New York. She is currently a writer-in-residence at Melbourne Theatre Company, developing *The Black Woman of Gippsland* from her grandmother's country. Her play, *Sunshine Super Girl*, about Wiradjuri tennis superstar Evonne Goolagong Cawley, was produced by Performing Lines and premiered in Griffith in October 2020 before travelling to the Sydney Festival. Her newest play is *Dogged*, written with collaborator and friend Cath Ryan.

From left: Jax Compton, Katina Olsen and Kyle Shilling in the Performing Lines/Griffith Regional Theatre 2020 production.
(Photo by Jamie James)

Andrea James

SUNSHINE SUPER GIRL

The EVONNE GOOLAGONG Story

CURRENCY PRESS
The performing arts publisher

CURRENCY PLAYS

First published in 2021
by Currency Press Pty Ltd,
Gadigal Land, Suite 310, 46-56 Kippax Street, Surry Hills, NSW 2010, Australia
enquiries@currency.com.au
www.currency.com.au

Reprinted 2022, 2023, 2024

Typeset by Dean Nottle for Currency Press.
Printed by CanPrint, Canberra, ACT.
Cover illustration and design by Emma Vine for Currency Press.

Currency Press acknowledges the Traditional Owners of the Country on which we live and work. We pay our respects to all Aboriginal and Torres Strait Islander Elders, past and present.

A catalogue record for this book is available from the National Library of Australia

Contents

Please note that this play contains offensive language.

Aboriginal readers are advised that this play makes reference to people who have died.

INTRODUCTION

Evonne Goolagong is Wiradjuri, a strong woman, a champion tennis player, a wonderful human, and my cousin.

Evonne, like me, is from the mighty Wiradjuri country. She was born in 1951 in Griffith and I was born later that decade in Leeton. Evonne grew up in Barellan; I grew up in Whitton, within an hour's drive of each other. Evonne's mother is my father's half-sister.

Growing up in South-Western NSW around that time had many challenges, particularly as young First Nation girls. We weren't sure what our futures would hold, what life challenges would come our way, or how we would come to terms with our own identity.

Wiradjuri country is the largest Aboriginal nation in NSW and one of the largest in Australia. The land occupies the plains running north and south-west of the Blue Mountains. The area was known as 'the land of the three rivers'—the Wambool, later known as the Macquarie, the Kalare, later known as the Lachlan, and the Murrumbidgee.

We spent our days swimming in rivers, fishing, exploring gum trees, and spending time with family, and always thinking: what is my future?

Evonne's future, as we know, would be on the world tennis stage, where she became a world champion, a national icon and national name—a proud Wiradjuri woman.

Evonne lived next door to the Barellan War Memorial Tennis Club courts. The town I grew up in has a memorial tennis club too and many hours were spent on those clay courts.

As Aboriginal people we faced widespread discrimination, particularly in rural Australia. However, Evonne had her tennis to focus on. People in the town were encouraged to play and when young Evonne was caught peering through the fence at the local courts, her path was set.

In March 1962, when we were still both young girls and probably didn't understand the significance of the change or what, if any, impact it would have on our lives, the Menzies government granted Aboriginal and Torres Strait Islander people the right to enrol to vote. I only learnt the significance of this change many years later, for while the right was there, enrolment and voting did not become compulsory for everyone who was eligible until 1984.

In 1965, life for Evonne was about to change. Our mob talk a lot about the bush telegraph—it's a way of life in the Indigenous community, a way of communication, a way to stay in touch, the way we got our news. However, on this occasion news of Evonne and her tennis talent had reached way beyond the bush telegraph to Sydney. Word reached Mr Vic Edwards, proprietor of a tennis school in Sydney, that this was a girl to watch. Vic travelled to Barellan to find out for himself and, as they say, the rest is history!

Eight years later, I followed in Evonne's footsteps to complete my education at Penrith High School. Although we both studied in Sydney, with Evonne finishing her schooling at Willoughby Girls High School, the question still pressing on us as two young Indigenous girls from South-Western NSW was what is our future?

The Sydney years

How life can take a turn, sometimes for the better and sometimes for the worse. In Evonne's case it is hard to say it was anything but for the better—going from a young koori girl growing up in the bush to living in the 'big smoke', going to a big school and learning to play tennis every day. Tennis would take her to the top of her sport, to become the national icon I spoke of earlier.

She was remarkable and so admired.

But Evonne was still a young woman, living away from home, away from her family and away from the surroundings of friendly Barellan.

With the familiar dirt grounds of the south-west replaced by the streets of suburban Sydney, the rivers replaced by a harbour, kangaroos, emus, lizards, snakes and cockatoos replaced by domestic pets, life couldn't have been more different for a young girl from the bush.

My own experience of moving to Sydney at the age of 16 was a difficult transition, with all those familiar smells, sounds and the fresh air from home all of a sudden gone. While I was still coming to terms with what my future held, Evonne's career was about to take off.

In 1967, when Evonne was 16 and I was just hitting double digits in age, the country held a referendum that allowed for Indigenous people to be included in the census. Imagine—Evonne was just four years away from winning her first Grand Slam title and had it not been for the referendum, Evonne would have not been counted as a citizen of this country. It was a bit like playing a kids' game of counting numbers but skipping one along the way.

The year 1971

Evonne had already had much success, here in Australia and at tournaments in England, Wales, West Germany and New Zealand. But 1971 was arguably when most of Australia and rest of the tennis world got to know or hear of Evonne Goolagong for the first time. That year Evonne lost the Australian Open to Margaret Court—another great Australian Tennis champion—in an epic three-set match: 6-2, 6-7, 5-7.

It was an era like no other. We had Ken Rosewall, men's champion; Margaret Court, women's champion defeating Evonne; John Newcombe and Tony Roche, men's doubles champions; and Evonne Goolagong and Margaret Court as women's doubles champions. They are remembered as the glory years of Australian tennis.

In 1971, I was at Leeton High School, being made to feel embarrassed and ashamed of my Aboriginality, while Evonne was heading for great success, winning tournaments and representing Australia at the highest of levels.

She won the first of her two Wimbledon titles in 1971 and went on to win her second title in 1980, a remarkable nine years after her first title win, beating four top-10 players and defeating two Grand Slam finalists in earlier rounds along the way. Her 1980 win made her the first mother to win Wimbledon since Dorothea Chambers in 1914. That same year I was in my first year of teaching at Lethbridge Park Primary School.

Evonne's career was so amazing to watch for many Australians—this young Indigenous girl from the bush, Wiradjuri country, born in Griffith, and grown up in Barellan, a town that had a population of 538 on the night of the 2016 census.

Who would have thought that this young girl from Barellan would go on to win 82 singles titles, 53 doubles titles and six mixed doubles titles? Her career also meant playing against some of the greatest players of her era, including Margaret Court, Martina Navratilova, Chris Evert and many others. It is a proud record and a wonderful career for a national icon—someone for many of us to look up to.

For me as a young girl growing up on Wiradjuri country, watching Evonne's career gave me and many others faith that there was a future, a career. I thank her for giving so many of us hope.

I am so glad to see this moving and funny play celebrating Evonne's life being staged and published; *Sunshine Super Girl* is both a gripping story and a great testament to the woman and her career. I have no doubt it will be enjoyed by many and will help a new generation learn of and be encouraged by all that she achieved.

My Wiradjuri cousin, you have been an inspiration to many. You played against and beat the best tennis players of your time and reached the height of your chosen career, from those humble beginnings in Barellan.

Congratulations on this wonderful play written in your honour—to one strong Wiradjuri woman, Evonne Goolagong, from another, Linda Burney MP.

Linda Burney
October 2020

Hon Linda Burney MP is the Federal Member for Barton, NSW. She was the first Aboriginal person to serve in the NSW Parliament in 2003 and the first Aboriginal woman elected to the Federal House of Representatives in 2016.

AUTHOR'S NOTE

Sunshine Super Girl: The Evonne Goolagong Story was independently commissioned through a Create NSW Aboriginal Arts Fellowship in 2016 that enabled me to extensively research material; travel throughout Wiradjuri Country and visit Evonne's home town of Barellan. Everyone I speak to about Evonne lights up at the memory of her bursting onto our television screens and newspaper back pages when she won the Wimbledon Open at just nineteen years of age in 1971. She was a joy to watch and was renowned for her grace both on and off the court. We were and remain so proud of our Australian tennis star who was a breath of fresh air on a sometimes stuffy tennis circuit. She superseded race and class barriers to become a number one tennis player and her legacy continues to this day.

Produced by the wonderful team at Performing Lines, the project underwent a series of creative developments in 2017, 2018 and 2019 to carefully nurture the story; and develop a dance language married with the text, that could emulate the flow and brilliance of a world class tennis player. Choreographer Vicki Van Hout was instrumental to this development journey and applied her rigorous practice to bring physical prowess to the storytelling through dance.

This play is based on a true story and has been dramatised for the stage. Research references include *Home: the Evonne Goolagong Story* by Evonne Goolagong Cawley and Phil Jarratt, *Evonne* by Evonne Goolagong and Bud Collins with Victor Edwards, *The Inner Game of Tennis* by W. Timothy Gallwey and *String Theory* by David Foster Wallace as well as archival materials from the Australian Film and Television Archive and The Wimbledon Tennis Library.

Francesca Smith gave me vital dramaturgical support as the play was forming and I also brought the work to Playwriting Australia's First Nations Writer's Retreat at Bundanon, where I was further dramaturgically guided by Raimondo Cortese, Louise Gough and Mari Lourey in a culturally driven peer to peer environment.

Many creatives have contributed to the development of the play, bringing their skill and intellect to the studio to finesse and refine the story and develop the physical language. Thank you to Bee Cruse, Guy Simon, Colin Kinchela, Taree Sansbury, Bjorn Stewart, Phoebe Grainger, Kirk Page, Chenoa Deemal, Lee Lewis and Rarriwuy Hick.

I have been ably mentored by Paige Rattray and must also give thanks to Narelle Lewis who was my initial producer at Performing Lines and a champion for the work. Many thanks to my partner and good friend Arnum Endean who gifted me Evonne's autobiography for my birthday and gave me the initial spark.

Finally, a special thank you to Evonne Goolagong-Cawley and her husband Roger Cawley who have generously given this play their critical eye and remain an inspiration.

Andrea James

Katie Beckett (left) and Kyle Shilling in the Performing Lines/Griffith Regional Theatre 2020 production. (Photo by Jamie James)

Sunshine Super Girl was produced by Performing Lines, and first presented by Griffith Regional Theatre on Wiradjuri Country, at West End Sports Stadium, Griffith, on 7 October 2020, with the following cast:

EVONNE	Katie Beckett
DAD KENNY, MR KURTZMAN, MR DUNLOP, BOB, ROGER, ITALIAN MEN, UMPIRE, REPORTER, PRESS 3, WIMBLEDON OFFICIAL	Kyle Shilling
LARRY, MR EDWARDS, LADY PLAYER 2, TED TINLING, SOUTH AFRICAN SERVANT, UMPIRE, PRESS 2	Luke Carroll
MUM LINDA, PATRICIA, ITALIAN MEN, SOUTH AFRICAN MAID, MARTINA NAVRATILOVA, PEACHES, JOHN NEWCOMBE	Jax Compton
BARBARA, MRS MARTIN, LADY PLAYER 1, ISABEL, PRESS 1, ITALIAN MEN, TENNIS ANGEL/ MARGARET COURT, OFFICIAL, CECIL	Katina Olsen

REPORTER and OFFICIALS are played interchangeably by the ensemble.

Writer and Director, Andrea James
Movement Director and Additional Choreography, Katina Olsen
Composition and Sound Design, Gail Priest
Lighting Design, Karen Norris
Video Media Design, Mic Gruchy
Set and Costume Design, Romanie Harper
Set and Costume Realiser, Melanie Liertz
Dramaturg, Louise Gough
Mentor, Paige Rattray
Original Choreographic Concept and Initial Movement Direction, Vicki Van Hout
Acting Coach, Shakira Clanton
Understudy, Mathew Cooper

CHARACTERS

The cast consists of five performers with roles distributed as follows:

Actor One	EVONNE
Actor Two	DAD KENNY, MR KURTZMAN, MR DUNLOP, BOB, ROGER, ITALIAN MEN, UMPIRE, REPORTER, PRESS 3, WIMBLEDON OFFICIAL
Actor Three	LARRY, MR EDWARDS, TED TINLING, LADY PLAYER 2, ITALIAN MEN, SOUTH AFRICAN SERVANT, UMPIRE, PRESS 2
Dancer One	MUM LINDA, PATRICIA, ITALIAN MEN, SOUTH AFRICAN MAID, MARTINA NAVRATILOVA, PEACHES, JOHN NEWCOMBE
Dancer Two	BARBARA, MRS MARTIN, LADY PLAYER 1, ISABEL, PRESS 1, ITALIAN MEN, TENNIS ANGEL / MARGARET COURT, OFFICIAL, CECIL

REPORTER and OFFICIALS are played interchangeably by ensemble members.

SETTING

The set is a tennis court, orange clay, and a high-rise umpire's chair. Some fruit boxes standing on end make do for the players' seating. There is a crude string net with an emu feather woven into it here and there. Two clothes lines either end. One line with a big, white bed sheet and the other with a few tiny 1970s tennis dresses and frilly undies fluttering in the air. The audience is seated along two sides in a traverse arrangement.

ACT ONE

ON COUNTRY

PROLOGUE—CENTRE COURT FISHING

Darkness. We hear the sound of a tennis match and commentary. It's the closing stages of a tie-breaker between Evonne Cawley and Chris Evert-Lloyd. We hear the 'toc, toc, toc' of the tennis ball and classic 1980s TV tennis commentary.

Lights very, very slowly illuminate a brilliant tennis court. Luminescent green. A holy grail. The sounds of the tennis game and commentary become louder and louder. The audience cheers.

EVONNE GOOLAGONG CAWLEY *enters with a suitcase and wicker fishing basket. Returning to Country, she looks around, puts down the suitcase, ascends the umpire's chair and throws a hand line into the court.*

Silence.

EVONNE: This is a good spot here. This is Mum's spot.
That current there? Swirling around and around? That's the backwater. Leaves and twigs and bugs. That's what the fish are after and that's what I'm after.
The fish.
My dad told me about the magic of fishing at the backwater.
He used to say, 'See that big hole down there? Plenty of fish. Big ones. That's where you go to catch a fish.'
But to tell you the truth, if I don't catch a fish, that's okay too …
No-one knows I'm here. Not even family. I'm not ready to go into town. Just yet.
Yesterday I fished around the corner. A bit closer to the bend and I caught three fish! Yellow belly and cod.
One pan size, one baking dish size and one family size.
Caught 'em on some worms. Took me two hours.

She smells her fingers.

Still got that fishy smell. It's starting to sink in.
Look out!

A fish bites. She scrambles to hook it, but misses.

Missed him!
Freshwater woman, through and through.
When I throw in a line and I'm waiting for a bite, it's like I'm on the court.
In the zone.
Your hearing changes—like you're underwater.
Your muscles shift and tighten. Ready for anything.
Your vision is sharp. Every twitch, every flutter.
And when everything aligns, that ball moves in slow motion and comes up to meet you.
Like an old friend.
And when you hit that sweet spot:
'Toc'!
It's like pure heaven.
That ball flies like a bird.
You watch your opponent scramble and before she hits the ball.
Wham!
You're there. You know where to be.

She winds in her line, gets down from the umpire's chair, walks to the centre of the court and picks up a handful of Wiradjuri dirt.

But why did I win, when so many others have lost?
What did it cost?
Why me?

SCENE 1: MANGY BALL

A car horn sounds. KENNY, LARRY *and* BARBARA *join* EVONNE *in the car.*

EVONNE: I'm three years old and we're travelling on a dirt road back from town to our little tin shack, when suddenly … Dad's car conks out.

ALL: Ohhhhhh.

KENNY: Don't worry, kids. I'll get it fixed in a jiffy. Barbara, you steer.

BARBARA *hops in the front to steer and* KENNY *pushes the car.*

That's it, my girl. [*Puff, pant*] Now turn her gently to the right. To the right! That's it. [*Puff, pant*] Now brakes, Barbara. Brakes!

EVONNE: And little Larry, quick as a whip, jumps in the front, gets down on the floor and pushes the brake pedal with his hand.

The car thankfully stops.

KENNY: Good girl, Barbara. Good boy, Larry. That's my boy.

KENNY *lifts the car bonnet and tinkers.* LARRY *and* BARBARA *amuse themselves by the side of the road.*

EVONNE: And here I am. In the middle of the bush, under a gum tree in Dad's big dusty old car. Spattered shade. Cicadas singing. The warm wind shuffling the long yellow grass. There's a grasshopper on the back window. We commune.

KENNY: Larry, come and hold this hammer for a minute. Don't lose those clips!

EVONNE: I put my grimy little hand into the back of the backseat and explore the universe there …

The DANCERS *dance the universe and bring objects to* EVONNE.

A spring.

A daddy-long-legs spider.

A coin.

A matchbox.

A newspaper.

Some fluff.

And then …

A DANCER *puts a grimy old tennis ball into* EVONNE*'s hand. She lifts it high into the air.*

My little treasure.

Round and small.

Abandoned from previous owners.

Kinda brown and bald.

I hold that ball and squeeze it tight.

KENNY *slams the bonnet down.*

KENNY: Come on, kids, let's go!

KIDS: Good one, Dad!

EVONNE: And then we're off! Barbara's in the front. Hair flying and Larry sets his eye on my treasure.

LARRY: What's that?

EVONNE: It's mine!

And I squeeze it and squeeze it and never let it go all the way till we get back home.

SCENE 2: BALL ON TIN

The PLAYERS *wheel in a corrugated iron wall.* LARRY *hits the tennis ball against the wall with a broomstick with a clang clang clang.* EVONNE *joins him and they take turns to hit the ball against the wall.*

LARRY: First one to hit five without missing wins!

EVONNE: Okay.

Our little shack with the tin walls and dirt floor was a bit rough around the edges, but it was my first home. I don't remember it much …

Evonne's mum, LINDA, *enters with a washing basket and hangs a white sheet on the clothes line.*

LINDA: Evonne! Larry! You've been at it all day! Will you find somewhere else to play with that ball?!

LARRY: First one to hit ten without missing wins.

EVONNE: Okay.

KENNY: Evonne! Larry! Will you take that game somewhere else?! You're driving ya mother and me spare!

LINDA: Has anyone seen my broom?

LARRY: Yeah, Dad! In a minute! First one to hit twelve without missing wins!

EVONNE: Wins what?

LARRY: I dunno! Nothing. Just wins the game.

EVONNE: Okay.

LINDA: I said, has anyone seen my …?

She spots the broom and grabs it off LARRY.

There it is!

EVONNE: Dad was away working. Shearing mainly.

KENNY *and the* DANCERS *enter.* KENNY *gun shears three sheep then and there.*

My dad set the Riverina shearing record. He could shear two hundred and twelve sheep a day for three years running, so I guess that's where I get my competitive streak from, ay?

EVONNE *gets a rusty shovel and a stick off the ground.* KENNY *sits off to the side and whittles away at some wood.*

LARRY: First one to hit fifteen without missing wins!
EVONNE: Okay!

The clang doosh clang clang doosh clang goes up a notch.

We play and play till the sun goes down and we have to squint to see the ball.
LINDA: Evonne! Larry! Get inside! Ya dinner's gone cold!

They stop playing and LARRY *runs inside.*

KENNY *hands* EVONNE *a crude wooden bat.*

KENNY: Evonne! Here ya go, love.
EVONNE: Thanks, Dad!

She hugs her little bat and ball.

My first tennis racquet made out of the side of a wooden fruit box from the picking.

A car approaches.

LINDA: Kids, get inside. Get inside the hut. Get inside now!

The KIDS *rush into the shack.* LINDA *keeps watch for the car.*

EVONNE: They were happy times at Tharbogan. But all us kids knew to look out for the black car. We had it drummed into us.

The black car …

It scared us to death!

LINDA *exits into the shack.*

So we move to Barellan. Wheat-belt country.

Between Binya and Moombooldool on Wiradjuri land.

SCENE 3: BARELLAN

KENNY, LINDA, LARRY *and* BARBARA *stack a pile of fruit boxes and sit in the car.*

EVONNE: Dad's shearing boss, Frank Gladman, helped Dad buy our own house in Barellan. But we can't get there because Dad's car broke down. Again!

ALL: Ohhhhhhhh!

LARRY: Shame job, Dad!

KENNY: I'll fix this car up in a jiffy.

EVONNE: So Mr Gladman tows us in the car behind his ute.

There was Dad at the wheel, Mum and little Kevin just two months old, Barbara and me squished in between; with Larry on Barbara's lap and all our worldly possessions in the back, piled up high.

LARRY: Proper shame job!

KENNY: Here we are!

They pile out of the car and LARRY, LINDA, KENNY *and* BARBARA *unload the boxes.*

EVONNE: This house is like a palace! It's an old shopfront in the main street with lino floorboards, a kitchen and two bedrooms, with electricity! We're proper 'uptown blackfellas' now!

LARRY: Evonne! Check this out!

LARRY *turns the lights on and off, on and off, on and off.* LINDA *slaps his hand.*

LINDA: Stop it! You'll blow up the electricity! We only just moved in!

LARRY *runs to the back of the house.*

LARRY: Evonne! Barbara! Come check this out!

EVONNE *and* BARBARA *join* LARRY.

EVONNE: The shopfront used to house the *Barellan Leader* newspaper and in the back room is the old printing press. It's a second-hand Double Royal that was transported from Cootamundra, but fell off the back of the truck and died. It's never printed a single newspaper! But it doesn't take long for the 'Goolagong Three' to make the local news …

LARRY: Let's check out the backyard!

LARRY *and* BARBARA *run outside to the backyard.*

EVONNE: We don't have any running water in our new house, but we don't care! We have a water tank outside with fresh rainwater! And out the back is a *sit-down* toilet! And out beyond that …

LARRY and BARBARA: [*together*] Evonne!

LARRY: Come out here!

LARRY and BARBARA: [*together*] Check this out!

EVONNE *joins* LARRY *and* BARBARA.

EVONNE: And beyond our outdoor dunny was the Barellan War Memorial Tennis Club courts! Right out the back! Next to our backyard!

SCENE 4: EVONNE'S WALL

BARBARA *and* LARRY *wheel in a corrugated iron water tank.* EVONNE *hits her ball against it with her wooden bat, tentatively learning the strokes.* BARBARA *and* LARRY *help her and hit the ball against the tank with the familiar and noisy clang, clang, clang.*

EVONNE: Backhand …

Forehand … Forehand.

Backhand.

Every night after school and during the weekends, I'd hit the ball with my fruit-box bat.

Backhand …

Forehand … Forehand.

Backhand …

Up against the butcher shop wall, the fence in our backyard, the water tank and the brick chimney.

Backhand …

Forehand … Forehand.

Backhand …

Our neighbours at Barellan are Mr and Mrs Dunlop! Dunlop! I'm not making this up!

MR DUNLOP *appears over the fence and waves.*

MR DUNLOP: Hello, Evonne!
EVONNE: Hello, Mr Dunlop!
MR DUNLOP: That forehand is looking pretty good.
EVONNE: Thanks, Mr Dunlop!
MR DUNLOP: I tell you what. To get your backhand up to speed, how about I lend you my tennis racquet?
EVONNE: Really?!
MR DUNLOP: Here ya go, love.

MR DUNLOP *gives* EVONNE *the tennis racquet and it immediately improves her play.*

EVONNE: Thanks, Mr Dunlop!
Wow!

LINDA *yells from the back door.*

LINDA: Evonne! Barbara! Larry! Bedtime!

LINDA *spreads out a bed sheet and* BARBARA, EVONNE *and* LARRY *jump in head to toe and fight for the blankets.*

EVONNE: Mum! Can I play in the tournament with Barbara and Larry tomorrow?
LARRY: She's too little!
EVONNE: No I'm not! Larry! Stop pulling the blankets!
LINDA: You can go and watch!
EVONNE: I don't wanna watch, I wanna play!
LINDA: Wait till you're older …
EVONNE: Pleaaaase?
BARBARA: Larry, give the blankets back!
LINDA: You haven't got any tennis sneakers.
EVONNE: I'll wear bare feet!
LINDA: Money's a bit tight at the moment.
EVONNE: So! Larry! Stop pulling the blankets.
BARBARA: And she's got no tennis dress!
EVONNE: I'll wear my tennis shoes.
LINDA: Darling, I haven't got any material left and Dad's work is a bit quiet at the moment.
EVONNE: Please. Pretty please … I'll be good.
LARRY: Barbara! Stop hogging the blankets!

BARBARA: Am not!
LINDA: And where are we gonna get your tennis shoes from?
EVONNE: We can borrow some off the Irvins. Please?
BARBARA: We've already borrowed off the Irvins.
EVONNE: Pretty pleeeeeeeeeeeeease?!
BARBARA: Shame job. Larry!
LARRY: Barbara!
EVONNE: Stop hogging the blankets.
LINDA: Be quiet, you lot! I've got an idea.

LINDA *pulls the top sheet off the bed!*

BARBARA: Hey!
LARRY: Muuuum!
EVONNE: Where ya going?!

LINDA *exits.*

Those blankets itch and scratch us all night and we never fought over the blankets again. Mum stayed up, tinkering away at something, I could hear her shuffling across the lino to put another log in the potbelly to keep her fingers working. Next morning …

LINDA *enters with a tennis dress.*

LINDA: Larry, Barbara, you're taking Evonne to the tennis! Barbara, go next door and borrow a pair of sneakers off the Dunlops.
BARBARA: Ohh?!
LINDA: Go on!
EVONNE: Yes!

The DANCERS *dress* EVONNE *in her borrowed shoes and her bed-sheet tennis dress.*

EVONNE: In 1956 I join the Barellan War Memorial Tennis Club. They have to make an age exemption.
I'm seven years old.

SCENE 5: PRINCESS

EVONNE *sneaks a magazine out of Barbara's sports bag and reads the front cover.*

EVONNE: *Princess—A Magazine for Girls.*

She turns the pages and pictures of white girls holding puppies, white girls holding bouquets, white girls sewing and white girls on showjumping ponies are projected onto the bed sheets.

Page one. Macramé.

Page two. Ponies.

Page three. Darning.

Page four. Ponies.

Page five. Enid Blyton.

Who?

Page six. More ponies.

Page seven. The Princess Club.

A tennis racquet!

Tennis!

A TENNIS ANGEL *with long legs appears, dressed in a white dress with black polka dots.*

Our Princess of the Week is Miss Jacqueline Monaghan of Coventry. Jacqueline likes collecting stamps, riding horses and playing tennis. Once a week, Jacqueline's mother takes her to train at the Wimbledon All England Tennis Club. Jacqueline hopes that one day she will play in the Wimbledon Junior Tournament on the all-famous Wimbledon Centre Court. Good luck, Jacqueline!

Wimbledon Centre Court.

The TENNIS ANGEL *exits whilst dancing a series of expert serves and volleys.* EVONNE *watches her in awe.*

Wimbledon Centre Court.

SCENE 6: MY OWN LITTLE TOURNAMENT

LARRY *and* BARBARA *join* EVONNE *on the tennis court and dance a fun game with each other. It's skilful and enjoyable to watch. When the dance ends they run to the net, shake hands, receive their trophies and pose for the cameras.*

An article from the Narrandera newspaper is projected onto the bed sheets.

REPORTER: Without doubt the most crowd-pleasing players were the Goolagong children: Barbara, Yvonne and Lance (tiny tots) playing with the skill of adults and getting all the fun in the world from their tennis.

EVONNE: We won the Narrandera Championships! Poor Larry! The paper called him Lance and we teased him with that name for weeks. Lance!

Everyone laughs.

LARRY: Shut up, Evonne! With a *'Y'*!

EVONNE: It's Evonne with an *'E'*!

LINDA *takes the trophies and puts them up on the shelf in the lounge room.*

A whistle sounds out. EVONNE *and the* DANCERS *perform a series of tennis drills. The drills are military in their precision.*

The Goolagong Three are becoming legendary and word has gotten down to the famous Victor A. Edwards Tennis School in Sydney. The Club President Mr Kurtzman lobbies for the school to come to Barellan to run a regional tennis clinic.

About one hundred kids come from the surrounding towns and we fill up the whole four courts.

We do this warm-up drill for two days! Solid.

For the Victor A. Edwards Tennis School, it's all about footwork and strokes. Endless repetitions. We haven't even hit a single ball!

A phone rings and MR EDWARDS *picks it up.* MRS MARTIN, *the coach in Barellan, is calling. On each side of the net is a different world. Barellan, hot, orange, windy and dusty; and Sydney, green, lush and luxurious.* EVONNE *and her* TEAMMATES *continue the movement drill in Barellan.*

MRS MARTIN: Mr Edwards. It's Faith here.

MR EDWARDS: Faith! How's it going at Barellan?

MRS MARTIN: Good! We've got about one hundred kids.

MR EDWARDS: Excellent.

MRS MARTIN: I think there's a young girl here you should come up and see.

MR EDWARDS: What?!

MRS MARTIN: A young girl. Could you come out and see her?

MR EDWARDS: Barellan?! That's miles away. I've got a lot on, Faith.

MRS MARTIN: Mr Edwards. She's pretty good.

MR EDWARDS: 'Pretty good'? How old is she?

MRS MARTIN: Nine.

MR EDWARDS: Nine years old! You want me to drive for seven hours to see a nine-year-old?

MRS MARTIN: It's just that …

MR EDWARDS: Wait till she can see over the net first!

MRS MARTIN: Mr Edwards, it's just that …

MR EDWARDS: I've gotta go …

MRS MARTIN: Vic! I mean, Mr Edwards. It's not just me. Colin Swan, the other coach, thinks the same.

MR EDWARDS: What? What did Colin say?

MRS MARTIN: There's something about this girl. The way she moves. Her instincts. We'll only be here for two more days. I think you should come out and see her.

MR EDWARDS: Yeah well …

MRS MARTIN: I think it'll be worth your while, Mr Edwards. You won't regret it.

Pause.

MR EDWARDS: Well, she'd better be bloody good.

MRS MARTIN: Great!

MR EDWARDS: I'll get Mrs Edwards to reschedule the coaching.

MRS MARTIN: And there's just one more thing?

MR EDWARDS: Hurry up.

MRS MARTIN: The girl?

Beat.

She's dark.

MR EDWARDS: Dark?!

MRS MARTIN: She's an Aboriginal girl.

MR EDWARDS: Ohhhhhh? Interesting …

SCENE 7: MR *KURTZMAN AND MEETING MARGARET*

MR KURTZMAN *arrives in his car.*

MR KURTZMAN: Morning, Evie.

EVONNE *jumps into his car.*

EVONNE: Mr Bill Kurtzman is the President of the Barellan War Memorial Tennis Club. He and Clarrie and Dot Irvin are my dedicated drivers. To build up my play, the Kurtzmans and the Irvins drive me all over the state of New South Wales to play the district championships.

MR KURTZMAN *hands* EVONNE *a new Dunlop-Slazenger racquet.*

MR KURTZMAN: Here ya go, love. For the Most Improved Player of the Year at the Barellan War Memorial Tennis Club!

EVONNE: My very own racquet!

MR KURTZMAN: We'll just swing in to get some petrol.

MR KURTZMAN *and* EVONNE *arrive at the petrol station.* CECIL DICKER *serves them.*

CECIL: G'day, Bill

MR KURTZMAN: G'day, Cecil. Fill her up!

CECIL *fills up the car.* MR KURTZMAN *gets out his map.*

EVONNE: I play the Girls Under 13 Championships and when I win all of those, I play the Under 18s.

LINDA *puts two trophies and a framed newspaper photo up on the lounge room shelf.*

We go to Leeton, Narrandera, Ganmain, Temora, Cowra and Young. We even go as far as Albury!

CECIL: Where you two off to today, Bill?

MR KURTZMAN: Me and this little champ are off to the Albury Tennis Club!

CECIL: Albury?!

MR KURTZMAN: Celebrating their fiftieth anniversary. They've invited our Evonne to play.

CECIL: Did they?!

EVONNE: Yep!

CECIL *and* MR KURTZMAN *are teasing* EVONNE *playfully.*

CECIL: She must be pretty good then!
MR KURTZMAN: Yeah, she must be!
CECIL: Not every day you get invited to play at the Albury Tennis Club.
MR KURTZMAN: That's right, Cecil!

CECIL *has put the petrol cap on.*

How much do I owe ya?
CECIL: It's on the house! Just make sure little Evie comes back with a trophy!
EVONNE: Thanks, Mr Dicker!

They drive off.

EVONNE *steps out of the car and onto the Albury tennis courts. The* TENNIS ANGEL *with the long legs and polka dot dress appears.*

That is the day I meet Margaret Smith. Who's Margaret Smith, ya say? Well, only the reigning Woman Champion of Wimbledon. 'Smith', who became 'Court'. I'm twelve years old and she's twenty-two.

The TENNIS ANGEL *performs the beautiful serve and volley dance; sidles up to* EVONNE, *whispers something into her ear and poses with* EVONNE *for the cameras.*

MR KURTZMAN *and* EVONNE *are back in the car driving home.* EVONNE *has her trophy on her lap.* MR KURTZMAN *chatters excitedly, nearly running off the road.*

MR KURTZMAN: What did she say to you, Evie?
Wo! What did she say?
EVONNE: She said …

Pause.

… 'Keep up the good work.'
MR KURTZMAN: 'Keep up the good work!' Margaret Smith! You met Margaret Smith! Wimbledon Champion! Here, have a sandwich.

He gives her a sandwich.

EVONNE: Thanks, Mr Kurtzman.
MR KURTZMAN: Show me your trophy!

EVONNE *proudly shows* MR KURTZMAN *her trophy.*

EVONNE: I won a red transistor radio!

MR KURTZMAN: That's the one! Evonne! You'll be playing the State Junior Championship before you know it! Wait till Mr Edwards hears about this! Haha!

He nearly runs off the road.

EVONNE and MR KURTZMAN: [*together*] Wo!

They laugh.

EVONNE: Just keep ya eyes on the road there, Mr Kurtzman!

MR KURTZMAN: That's the way, Evonne.

EVONNE: Mr Kurtzman, have you ever been to Wimbledon?

MR KURTZMAN: Phoar! Wimbledon! You gotta go into the lottery to get Centre Court tickets at Wimbledon. That's the golden ticket!

EVONNE: Wimbledon Centre Court.

EVONNE *hands the red transistor radio to* LINDA *who puts it up on the lounge room shelf.*

Next day, Dad drove us to the Condobolin Cinemas for a treat.

EVONNE, LARRY *and* BARBARA *sit in the front row of the cinema.*

We had to sit all the way up the front with the other black kids.

They strain their necks to see the screen.

We watched *Chitty Chitty Bang Bang* in DeLuxe Color!

The theme song pours out of the flickering screen. EVONNE, BARBARA *and* LARRY *rub their sore necks.*

SCENE 8: THAT'S MY GIRL

The Goolagongs' kitchen. There is a smart tablecloth on the table. LINDA, *wearing her best dress, pours tea for* MR EDWARDS. LINDA *is painfully shy and the conversation is awkward.*

MR EDWARDS: Lovely house you've got here, Mrs Goolagong.

LINDA: We like it.

MR EDWARDS: And the tennis courts! Just out the back! How about that?!

LINDA: Yes. The kids love it.

MR EDWARDS: Your daughter Evonne is a very good tennis player.

LINDA: As long as she's having fun.

MR EDWARDS: We haven't seen someone Evonne's age showing so much talent for quite some time.

LINDA *takes a photo of* EVONNE *off the wall.*

LINDA: This is Evonne after she won the tournament at Leeton.

MR EDWARDS: Mr Kurtzman keeps me updated.

LINDA: Very good man, Mr Kurtzman. He drives Evonne to all her tournaments.

MR EDWARDS: Mrs Goolagong. Evonne's outplayed her competition here.

LINDA: I see.

MR EDWARDS: She has the makings of a world champion. But for her to get any better she'd have to go to Sydney.

LINDA: I've never been to Sydney, Mr Edwards.

MR EDWARDS: There's some girls in Sydney that would really make Evonne stand up and play.

LINDA: I see. Sydney?

MR EDWARDS: We'd treat her like family. She can train with me and my daughter Patricia every day. She can come and live with us.

LINDA: Sydney's a long way, Mr Edwards.

MR EDWARDS *stands.*

MR EDWARDS: Your daughter is a very talented young lady, Mrs Goolagong.

LINDA: Yes. She is.

MR EDWARDS: Shame to see all that talent go to waste.

Beat.

Have a think about it, Mrs Goolagong.

MR EDWARDS *exits.*

EVONNE *enters. She's been listening in the next room. She quietly sits next to* LINDA *and puts her head on her shoulder.* LINDA *turns on the radio and they listen together.* LINDA *hugs* EVONNE *in the knowing that she will have to let her go to Sydney.*

SCENE 9: BARELLAN SUITCASE

A DANCER *brings a suitcase onto the court. She opens it.*

EVONNE: Everyone in the town of Barellan rallies to raise the money to get me to Sydney. Constable Bert Hammond forms a Fundraising Committee and Mr Kurtzman puts a donation tin in every shop in Barellan to cover my airfare and weekly expenses. I'm going on an airplane!

Mr Kurtzman asks Mrs Kurtzman to buy me a new suitcase and all the women of the town fill it up.

The DANCERS *fill the case with clothing and dress* EVONNE *in a red coat, hat and gloves.*

Mrs Irvin sewed me a shirt, Mrs Dunlop knitted me a cardigan and Mrs Gladman brought me a new red coat all the way from Griffith.

Mrs Jessie Douglas designed me a brand new tennis dress that Mum ran through the copper and Mr Kurtzman presented me with another brand new Slazenger tennis racquet.

MR KURTZMAN *presents* EVONNE *with the racquet. She holds it close to her chest.*

Mum, Dad, Barbara, Larry … Mr and Mrs Kurtzman, Mr Dicker, everyone drove to the Narrandera Airport to see me off.

A DANCER *closes the suitcase and they are at the airport.*

LINDA: Did you bring a fresh hankie?
EVONNE: Yes, Mum.
LINDA: Make sure you write.
EVONNE: I will. Let me know when the new baby comes.
LINDA: We will.
EVONNE: I hope it's a girl.
LINDA: It will be what it will be. You be good now.
EVONNE: I'm gonna get better.
LINDA: We know you will, love.

LINDA *hands* EVONNE *her red transistor radio.*

I thought you might like this.
EVONNE: Thanks, Mum!

LINDA: To keep ya company.

EVONNE *gives* LINDA *a long hug.*

Well, time to go.

EVONNE: I'll make you proud of me.

EVONNE *hugs and kisses her family and walks across the tarmac towards the plane. She waves one last goodbye and gets on the plane.*

SCENE 10: HEAD IN THE CLOUDS

EVONNE *is on the airplane, clutching her tennis racquet to her chest. The engines of the plane are very noisy.*

EVONNE: I look down and all the trees and the cows and the houses and dams are like tiny dots. And I can see our river!

The sun hits the water and it sparkles and shines like a jewel. Like a diamond tiara stretched right across the land. My childhood playground.

There's Griffith and the fringe camp at Tharbogan. To the left I spot Barellan and there's the tiny, tiny, tiny tennis courts and our house! And then there's Moombooldool and looking right back I can see the big lake up the top of Darlington Point—Mum's favourite fishing spot.

And we're going up and up and up and then we're in the clouds and I can't see nothing anymore. That's it. Giant cotton ball clouds, so close I can touch them. So white, they're making my eyes hurt.

I didn't know it then, but coming out of Sydney is a bus …

The DANCERS *drive a miniature bus on the lines of the tennis court.*

It's got 'Student Action for Aborigines' written on the side. On its way to Walgett and Kempsey, Bowraville and Moree.

And we're going up and up and up …

On the tail of the plane is a painted boomerang.

Will I be coming back?

END OF ACT ONE

ACT TWO

LIVING WHITE

SCENE 11: LIVING WHITE

EVONNE *is in her new bedroom seated on a Queen Ann bed. Girly wallpaper is projected onto the bed-sheet walls with the words 'Living white' overlaid. Her hair is wet and wrapped in a towel. A hairdryer lies next to her on the bed.*

EVONNE: Mr and Mrs Edwards have a giant house in Sydney. We go over the Harbour Bridge to get here. When Mrs Edwards stops at the tollgate and chucks in a twenty-cent coin I say:
'Gee, we don't have to pay to use the bridge at Barellan.'

The DANCERS *chuckle.*

Then I think, 'Shut up, Evonne!'
Then we pull up to this big white house with a big white fence out the front. And lawn! Like, real mowed lawn! And rose bushes! This house has got an upstairs and a downstairs!
[*Whispering*] Everything is very quiet.
I'm sharing this bedroom with Patricia. Patricia is Mr Edwards' younger daughter. We're gonna be doubles partners.

There's a tentative knock on the door.

PATRICIA: [*offstage*] Evonne.

EVONNE *doesn't answer.*

Evonne, are you okay?

PATRICIA *enters.*

You haven't dried your hair yet. Mum said! 'No wet hair during dinner.'

Pause.

Are you okay? I'm not cross about you being in my room. I love having a room mate.

Beat.

EVONNE: Trisha, I've never used an electric hairdryer before.

PATRICIA *giggles.*

PATRICIA: What?!

EVONNE: I don't even know how to turn it on!

EVONNE *giggles too. They both start laughing.*

PATRICIA: Why didn't you say?! Here, let me dry your hair.

EVONNE *takes the towel off her head.*

Oh my god! Your hair is so curly!

PATRICIA *turns on the hairdryer and dries* EVONNE*'s hair.*

EVONNE: That night I lay awake in the dark. I can hear the buzz of the city. A hum, that never goes away. The cars. A creak on the stairs. A glow in the sky.
When I look out the window …
I can't see the stars …

SCENE 12: IN TRAINING

EVONNE *is on the court.* MR EDWARDS *is feeding her tennis balls as she practises her repetition strokes.*

MR EDWARDS *starts feeding the balls harder, making her run from one side of the court to the other.*

MR EDWARDS *feeds the balls faster.*

EVONNE *starts to tire.*

MR EDWARDS: [*yelling*] What's wrong with you? Do you need a chair?!

EVONNE: No!

MR EDWARDS *feeds more balls.* EVONNE *picks up her pace.*

MR EDWARDS: If you wanna be a world champion. And that's my intention! You'll have to run after every ball! You got that?

EVONNE: Yep.

MR EDWARDS: We've enrolled you into Willoughby Girls High.

EVONNE: Uhuh.

MR EDWARDS: And elocution lessons with Madame Hagney.

EVONNE: Oh?

MR EDWARDS: A world champion does not mumble.

EVONNE: Yes, Mr Edwards.

MR EDWARDS: And we've gotta improve your strokes.

EVONNE: Yes, Mr Edwards.

MR EDWARDS: It's no good running everything down if you can't return it with a perfect stroke.

EVONNE: Yes, Mr Edwards.

MR EDWARDS: You've got a good backhand stroke. You've learnt well.

He feeds EVONNE *some backhand volleys.*

That's your secret weapon.

EVONNE: Yes, Mr Edwards

MR EDWARDS: You've gotta expose your opponent's weakness. You gotta watch her like a hawk. Serve, volley, run, backhand, forehand. Get yourself into position and let it work for you. Okay. You're ready now, for White City.

SCENE 13: WHITE CITY

PATRICIA *runs onto the court wearing a matching outfit and joins* EVONNE *in a warm up. Two* OLDER WOMEN *at the other side face off.* PATRICIA *and* EVONNE *have their competition finely honed. It's a beautiful dance. Accompanied by the 'toc toc' of tennis balls and polite applause. The* OLDER WOMEN *struggle to win and gain their composure. A* REPORTER *reports from the side.*

REPORTER: I saw yesterday a sight that will stay in my mind forever—a slim brown Aboriginal girl from the bush, playing tennis on a posh Sydney court, her face alive with delight … She may well become the first Aborigine to become champion of the world in any sport. Signing off. Frank Margan from the *Sydney Daily Telegraph*.

EVONNE *and* PATRICIA *win their game, polite applause.* EVONNE *and* PATRICIA *change ends.*

EVONNE: Actually, Lynch Cooper was the first Aboriginal World Champion. He won the Stawell Gift running race in 1929 and Lionel Rose is on his way with the boxing—he's my inspiration.

The press give me all sorts of nicknames. They call me:

REPORTER: 'Dusky'.

The names are projected around the court and EVONNE *prepares to serve.*

'The Champ with the Soft Brown Eyes'.

EVONNE: And …

Beat.

REPORTER: 'Biscuit-coloured'.

EVONNE: Biscuit-coloured?!

Anyway, doesn't matter, me and Trisha are playing these ladies in the Doubles Final. This is match point and I'm serving for the match.

EVONNE *serves and* PATRICIA *return volleys for the match. The audience applauds.*

Yes!

EVONNE *and* PATRICIA *run to the net in slow motion. Like a nightmare.*

I don't remember that woman's name, but I can remember her face and what she wore. She had these green buttons down her tennis dress and mousey-coloured hair that was clipped to one side. I think she might've even been wearing a bit of make-up. Her fringe was stuck to her forehead with sweat and she was wearing a wedding ring that flashed in the sun when she came into the net. When I shook her hand it was kinda limp, cold, damp …

EVONNE *and* PATRICIA *shake hands with the* WOMEN.

LADY PLAYER 1: Well, that's the first time I've ever had the pleasure of playing a *nigger*.

The word 'nigger' is projected around the court.

EVONNE: What?

Nigger?

SCENE 14: 'THE FOUNDY'

Disco lights. EVONNE *and the* DANCERS *are wearing disco clothes—and grooving along to some classic 60s Aboriginal rock.*

EVONNE: Thank God, there's the Foundation for Aboriginal Affairs in town. They have their headquarters in George Street. All the old uncles call it 'the one-stop shop'.

You can go in there for a coffee and if you're lucky Jimmy Little will serve you!

All the blackfellas who come into Sydney stop off at 'the Foundy'. You can grab a feed if you're hungry and some clothes and toys for the kids.

But the best thing of all are the weekend social dances.

Blackfellas come for miles for the socials. The mob hire a hall in Redfern or Alexandria and Mum Shirl is the bouncer out the front! She never lets anyone in who causes any trouble and look out if you muck up on the dance floor.

Yeah! Thank God for 'the Foundy'.

BOB *dances and twirls with* EVONNE.

I met Bob Morgan at 'the Foundy'—he jumped on the Freedom Bus when it came through Walgett and came to Sydney to work with Charlie Perkins.

ISABEL *joins them for a dance.*

And this is where I also meet my best friend Isabel. She's Arrente.

They're yelling over the music.

ISABEL: What did she call you?

EVONNE: A nigger!

ISABEL: A what?!

EVONNE: She called me a nigger!

BOB: Don't worry about it, Evie.

ISABEL: Nigger?!

BOB: You're the one that came home with the trophy!

EVONNE: No-one's ever said that to me before.

ISABEL: Yeah. Well, get used to it, sis.

EVONNE: I don't wanna get used to *that.*

BOB: Tell 'em to go get stuffed!

EVONNE: I'm not as political as you!

BOB: You're a blackfella living in Australia. That's political!

EVONNE: She wanted me to shrink. But I'm not playing that game.

ISABEL: Yeah!

BOB: Stuff that!

EVONNE: There's no winners in *that* game.

BOB: Come with us to the march next week, ay?

ISABEL: Yeah, come with us, Evie.

EVONNE: Whose gonna listen to a tennis player?

BOB: Come to the march.

EVONNE: I've got training. When I'm world champion, then they'll listen.

ISABEL: You can miss one day.

BOB: Come on, where do you stand?

EVONNE: I've got a tournament coming up in Europe. It's my *first* trip abroad.

BOB: Abroooooad?!

ISABEL: All fancy pants now that you live over the bridge.

BOB: In Rooooose-ville.

EVONNE: Haha.

BOB: Come to the march.

ISABEL: Yeah, can't expect us to fly the flag for you every time.

EVONNE: Sorry, Izzy.

BOB: [*teasing*] Well, when we get our land rights, I suppose we can give some of it back to Evonne, ay Isabel?

ISABEL: Yeah, 'spose!

They laugh and dance the night away.

END OF ACT TWO

ACT THREE

ON THE CIRCUIT

SCENE 15: THE INNER GAME OF TENNIS

EVONNE *is on the tennis court with* MR EDWARDS. *She's been practising for hours. It's a beautiful dance. A solo.*

VOICE-OVER: In order to anticipate how and where to move the feet and whether to take the racquet back on the forehand or backhand side, the brain must calculate within a fraction of a second the moment the ball leaves the server's racquet, approximately where it is going to land, and where the racquet will intercept it. Into this calculation must be computed the initial velocity of the ball, combined with an input for the progressive decrease in velocity and the effect of wind and of spin, to say nothing of the complicated trajectories involved. Then, each of these factors must be recalculated after the bounce of the ball to anticipate the point where contact will be made by the racquet. Simultaneously, muscle orders must be given—not just once, but constantly refined on updated information. Finally, the muscles have to respond in co-operation with one another; a movement of feet occurs, the racquet is taken back at a certain speed and height, and the face of the racquet is kept at a constant angle as the racquet and body move forward in balance. Contact is made at a precise point according to whether the order was given to hit down the line or cross-court—an order not given until after a split-second analysis of the movement and balance of the opponent on the other side of the net.

You have approximately .613 seconds to accomplish all this, but even if you are returning the serve of an average player, you have only about one second … to hit the ball is clearly a remarkable feat; to return it with consistency and accuracy is a mind-boggling achievement. Yet it is not uncommon. The truth is that everyone who inhabits a human body possesses a remarkable creation.

No computer yet made is capable of doing the calculations and giving the necessary muscle orders involved in returning a fast serve in the time required. *

SCENE 16: THE HOLY COURT

EVONNE *recovers. The court transforms to a luminescent glowing green ...* EVONNE *looks around her in awe.* LINDA *puts more trophies up on the lounge room shelf.*

EVONNE: And now, after winning eleven regional and city championships at home and getting runners-up at the Australian Open …
Here I am.
1970.
The Holy Court of The Holy Grounds. Tennis's most sacred site. The Wimbledon Green and the Perfect Whites. Manicured to perfection. Ivy walls, impeccable gardens, dressing-room attendants dressed like scientists and the strawberries and cream!
Nothing could have prepared me for the stiff tradition of Wimbledon.

She and her opponent, JANE 'PEACHES' BARTKOWICZ, *sit in a small corridor of light. There's a giant clock that tick-tocks noisily.*

I'm about to go onto Centre Court and I'm in this waiting room. A glass box kinda thing. You're just one yard away from your opponent. It's surreal. Nobody talks.

The PLAYERS *check each other out.* EVONNE *looks at the clock nervously. After some time an* OFFICIAL *enters and the* PLAYERS *stand. The* OFFICIAL *inspects the* PLAYERS.

Then they inspect your clothes, hair, shoes, to ensure that you are wearing …

OFFICIAL: … predominately white.

EVONNE: The waiting room is underneath the royal box. If there's royalty present a little blue light is switched on in the corridor.

A blue light flashes.

The light is on! And then, before you know it …

---

* from W. Timothy Gallwey, *The Inner Game of Tennis*.

OFFICIAL: Ladies. It's time.

PEACHES *and* EVONNE *stand.*

EVONNE: Over the doorway before you enter Centre Court is a poem:
'If you can meet with triumph and disaster,
And treat those two imposters just the same.'

Mum would love that saying.

The PLAYERS *walk out onto the court and take their seats. There is a hush in the air.*

And here I am. Eighteen years of age on the Holy Court of the Holy Grounds in the Second Round. Me, the newcomer, playing Jane 'Peaches' Bartkowicz from the United States.

The PLAYERS *take to the court.*

But why am I being pushed out onto Centre Court? Me and Peaches are both low-ranked players?

London got wind of the …

REPORTER: Aborigine girl from the outback!

EVONNE: I'm the Wimbledon Freak Show.

EVONNE *prepares to serve. She looks up to the crowd.*

There are 14,000 people seated around this court. Come to watch me play. There's more people here than the entire town of Barellan! More than Barellan, Griffith and West Wyalong combined!

EVONNE *and* PEACHES *dance.* EVONNE *serves and runs in to play, but freezes. She struggles while* PEACHES *is dancing about brilliantly. The clock and scoreboard click over quickly: 6-4 and 6-0 over 34 minutes. They shake hands at the net and then suddenly* EVONNE *is seated in front of the press. Bright lights flashing.*

PRESS 1,2 and 3: Miss Goolagong! Miss Goolagong!

PRESS 1: Miss Goolagong! Can you throw a boomerang?

EVONNE: What?

PRESS 3: Miss Goolagong. Do you feel proud to be the first Aborigine to play Wimbledon?

EVONNE: Well …

PRESS 1: Can you speak Aboriginal?

EVONNE: I …
PRESS 2: What do you think of apartheid?
PRESS 3: Will you be playing Arthur Ashe in the doubles?
PRESS 1: Come on, Evonne, one or two words in Aboriginal.
PRESS 1,2 and 3: Miss Goolagong! Miss Goolagong!
REPORTER: Dreamtime daughter of the outback crashes in the second round.

The headline 'Dreamtime daughter of the outback crashes in the second round' is projected around the court.

SCENE 17: NOT SUCH A LITTLE GIRL NOW

EVONNE *puts on a long skirt, gloves and handbag and the court transforms into the Wimbledon Ball replete with disco ball.*

EVONNE: The Wimbledon Ball in 1970 was a blast! There's Rod Laver! Billie Jean King. Arthur Ashe. Elton John and Cliff Richards! But this year it's an Aussie blitz!

The tennis angel MARGARET COURT, *dressed in a polka dot gown, enters the room with* JOHN NEWCOMBE, *holding their trophies to great applause.*

Margaret Court and John Newcombe have won the Men's and Women's Singles and they're leading the winners waltz. Good on you, Margaret, and 'Bewdy Newk'!

A cheesy song begins and MARGARET *and* NEWCOMBE *waltz awkwardly.*

EVONNE *watches from the side of the dance floor as* ROGER CAWLEY *enters and sidles up to her.*

ROGER: You're not going out for a dance?
EVONNE: No. I think I'll stand this one out.
ROGER: You've got a good backhand.
EVONNE: So they say.
ROGER: Really good.
EVONNE: Not good enough for me this year, I'm afraid.
ROGER: Peaches Bartkowicz.
EVONNE: Peaches! Knocked me off my perch. I'm Evonne …

ROGER: Goolagong! I know … I'm Roger. Roger Cawley.

They shake hands.

EVONNE: So you're not on the circuit anymore?

ROGER: Oh, you know about that?

EVONNE: I've heard a few things on the circuit.

ROGER: The men's competition is fierce.

EVONNE: So's the women's!

ROGER: Of course! I'm not saying …

EVONNE: You're alright! So what do you do now?

ROGER: Jack of all trades. I'm a check-in clerk at British Overseas and I do a bit of writing on the side.

EVONNE: A writer! What do you write?

ROGER: Oh, just a few things.

EVONNE: Like …?

ROGER: Oh. Nothing.

EVONNE: What do you write?

Pause.

ROGER: I write love stories.

Beat.

And poems.

EVONNE: Love stories!

MR EDWARDS *enters with a glass of cognac and a cigar. He's a bit tipsy.*

ROGER: On the side.

EVONNE: Oh?

ROGER: For women's magazines

EVONNE: I see.

ROGER: I'm saving to start up a business.

EVONNE: And you write love stories?

ROGER: It pays well.

MR EDWARDS *approaches.*

MR EDWARDS: Hello, Evonne. Having a good time?

EVONNE: Roger, this is my coach Mr Edwards. Roger Cawley.

ROGER *and* MR EDWARDS *shake hands.*

MR EDWARDS: I used to see you on the Juniors circuit.
ROGER: That's right.
MR EDWARDS: Oh. Right-o. [*To* EVONNE] Getting a bit late. We should get you home now. I'll just finish this drink and then we'll go.
EVONNE: I'd like to stay a little longer if that's okay?
MR EDWARDS: Young ladies shouldn't be seen out without a chaperone.
EVONNE: I'm eighteen years of age, Mr Edwards.
MR EDWARDS: Where's Patricia?
EVONNE: I think she stepped out for some fresh air.
ROGER: If Evonne and Patricia would like to stay, I'll make sure they get to a cab.
MR EDWARDS: My girls have an 11.30 p.m. curfew.
ROGER: I see.
MR EDWARDS: I'm going to find Patricia.

They watch him leave. EVONNE *looks out for* PATRICIA.

EVONNE: Where is she?
ROGER: Out on the balcony with my mate John!
EVONNE: Oh dear.
ROGER: John and Trish are going out dancing tomorrow. Shall we join them?
EVONNE: Maybe. We'll see.
ROGER: It'd be a shame to come all the way to London and not see some nightlife.

MR EDWARDS *enters, fuming.*

MR EDWARDS: Come on, Evonne! Let's go! Patricia is outside waiting for the car!
EVONNE: Good night, Roger.

MR EDWARDS *exits.*

ROGER: See you soon?

ROGER *exits and the court transforms into Evonne's hotel room.*

EVONNE: Back at the hotel, Patricia ran straight to her room. Mr Edwards spotted Patricia kissing John and gave her a serve!

MR EDWARDS *barges into Evonne's hotel room with a bottle of champagne.*

MR EDWARDS: Eeeeeeeeeeevie!

EVONNE: Isn't a bit late for a meeting?

MR EDWARDS: We gotta talk about South Africa.

EVONNE: South Africa?! I'm very tired, Mr Edwards.

MR EDWARDS: Don't worry. The minute there's any trouble we'll pack you up and take you back home.

EVONNE: Trouble?! Let's talk about this tomorrow.

MR EDWARDS: The South African tournament has sent you a written invitation.

EVONNE: It's been a big day, I should get some sleep.

MR EDWARDS: Gotta sort out a bit of paperwork. But she'll be right. [*Shouting*] Miss Evonne Goolagong! My champion!

EVONNE: Ssh, Mr Edwards! It's late!

MR EDWARDS: Tennis champion of the worrrrrrrrrld!

EVONNE: Mr Edwards! You'll wake the other guests!

MR EDWARDS *stumbles, holds up the bottle of champagne.*

MR EDWARDS: I brought us some champagne.

EVONNE: No thank you.

MR EDWARDS: To celebrate your first Wimbledon tour.

Pause.

Let me run you a bath, hey?

Pause.

EVONNE: Where's Mrs Edwards?

MR EDWARDS: Asleep.

EVONNE: You should go back to your room.

MR EDWARDS: Not such a little girl now, are you?

EVONNE: No. I'm not.

MR EDWARDS: Let me look at you.

EVONNE: It's been a big day, Mr Edwards, and I think …

MR EDWARDS: Not in the Juniors anymore …

EVONNE: No. I'm not.

MR EDWARDS: Quite the young lady now, aren't you?

EVONNE: My mother brought me up well.

MR EDWARDS: How about you pop yourself in the bath and I'll pour you a champagne?

He lurches towards her.

EVONNE: I don't think so!
MR EDWARDS: Ohhh, come on, Evie!

He chases her around the room.

EVONNE: No!
MR EDWARDS: Come on! Let me show you a few moves!
EVONNE: I said no!

She yells for someone to hear her.

Hello! Hello!
MR EDWARDS: Come on, baby! Let's dance …

He grabs EVONNE *and forces her to dance. She struggles against his grip.*

EVONNE: Get out!
MR EDWARDS: Oooh, feisty!
EVONNE: I said get out!

EVONNE *pushes him and he lands on his arse.*

MR EDWARDS: You ungrateful little …
EVONNE: You need to leave. Now!
MR EDWARDS: After all I've done for you.
EVONNE: I'll see you and Mrs Edwards at breakfast in the morning.

MR EDWARDS *stands and goes to exit, but then doubles back.*

MR EDWARDS: You know, you're like a daughter to me.

He goes to kiss EVONNE *on the cheek. She turns her head to avoid him. He grabs the unopened bottle of champagne and finally exits.*

SCENE 18: 'CHOCOLATO'

EVONNE *dresses and prepares for a date.*

EVONNE: The next day, Patricia, John, Roger and I go dancing. And then Roger follows that up with a single date.

The court transforms into a London pub.

He takes me to a rowdy London pub.

ROGER *enters with two drinks.*

ROGER: A gin and tonic and a juice for the lady!

He hands EVONNE *her drink.*

Welcome to my office!

EVONNE: Your office?!

ROGER: The old Half Moon Hotel!

EVONNE: It's beautiful!

ROGER: Cheers!

They clink glasses and sip.

EVONNE: We stay at the pub till stumps and talk the night away. I tell him about my family at home.

ROGER: You have *seven* brothers and sisters?

EVONNE: Yep! And *hundreds* of cousins. Maybe you'll meet them one day.

ROGER: I'd like that.

EVONNE: And then here I am. In Rome.

The court transforms into the Italian Open.

The beautiful Foro Italico.

Roger and his mate Fish followed us to Italy and they've been sneaking around the tournament trying not to be seen by Mr Edwards.

It seems this Roger Cawley is my lucky charm.

There's a lot of men watching this game today. Between each point I can hear a chorus of …

ITALIAN MEN: Chocolato! Chocolato!

EVONNE: When I win my match with an ace, the Italians go wild.

ITALIAN MEN: Chocolato! Chocolato!

EVONNE: The next day, to avoid Mr Edwards, Roger and I meet at the launderette.

At the laundrette EVONNE *is watching her tennis clothes spin in the dryer.* ROGER *sneaks in with a picnic basket.*

ROGER: Gong! Fancy meeting you here!

EVONNE: Mr Cawley! What a coincidence. Did you bring your washing?

ROGER: Yep! And I packed us a lunch!

EVONNE: Very romantic!

ROGER *lays out a picnic rug.*

ROGER: A good strong Italian coffee and my favourite cheese.

EVONNE *smells the cheese.*

EVONNE: Phewie!
ROGER: Monte Veronese. They make this in the mountains.
EVONNE: Smells to high heaven.
ROGER: Once you try this cheese, you will never look back. Just block your nose when you put it in your mouth.

EVONNE *blocks her nose and tastes the cheese.*

EVONNE: Mmmmmm. Not bad. Not like the Coon we have at home.
ROGER: The what?
EVONNE: The Coon.

ROGER *looks bewildered.*

Never mind.
ROGER: Here. Have a strawberry.

He pops a strawberry in EVONNE*'s mouth.*

EVONNE: Mmmmm. Not bad.

ROGER *pours the coffee.*

ROGER: How do you have your coffee?
EVONNE: I'm a cuppa tea kinda girl, myself.
ROGER: Take a sip of this. It'll knock your socks off.

They clink glasses.

EVONNE and ROGER: [*together*] Cheers!

EVONNE*'s eyes water.*

EVONNE: Wo!
ROGER: That'll keep you up all night.
EVONNE: I'm already awake all night!
ROGER: Me too.
EVONNE: I can't stop thinking about you, Mr Roger Cawley.
ROGER: I've never met anyone like you, Miss Evonne Goolagong.

They look at each other tenderly. Maybe they're about to kiss.

The dryer pings.

EVONNE: Oops! My clothes are ready.

EVONNE *hops up and takes her clothes out of the dryer.*

ROGER: Here. I'll give you a hand.

He picks up her frilly tennis knickers and quickly drops them.

Maybe not!

EVONNE: You keep your eyes off my knickers, Mr Cawley!

ROGER: I've seen them before.

She glares at him.

On the tennis court …

When you were …

Not that I was looking!

Pause.

EVONNE *folds her clothes. Little tennis dresses.*

EVONNE: I have to leave on Friday.

ROGER: I know. I'm gonna miss you, Evonne Goolagong.

EVONNE: I'm gonna miss you too, Mr Roger Cawley.

They kiss.

SCENE 19: VIC EDWARDS WRATH

EVONNE *runs on to the court and prepares for her training session.* MR EDWARDS *enters carrying a basket full of tennis balls and an arm full of racquets. He feeds balls to* EVONNE. *He's pissed off.* EVONNE *struggles to keep up.*

MR EDWARDS: I've been seeing a lot of that young Roger Cawley, lurking about the circuit.

EVONNE: Really?

MR EDWARDS: Yes.

He feeds more curve balls at her.

I thought he'd retired?

EVONNE: Well, yes …

MR EDWARDS: Now let that wrist relax! This forehand will be your undoing if you don't watch it.

EVONNE: I've got it.

MR EDWARDS: Relax! You're playing Julie Heldman today. Californian girl. Tennis royalty. Her dad was a junior champion and her mum founded a tennis magazine. If you play your cards right in this match, we'll get you to the quarters at Wimbledon this year.

EVONNE: Yes, Mr Edwards.
MR EDWARDS: I've got a good feeling about Wimbledon.
EVONNE: I won't let you down, Mr Edwards.

MR EDWARDS *stops feeding her balls.*

MR EDWARDS: Good. Take a break. Drink plenty of fluids and remember what I told you.

EVONNE *sits down to recover.* MR EDWARDS *sits down and puts his hand on her knee.*

You know, if it's boys you're interested in …

EVONNE *takes his hand off her knee, stands up and packs her things.*

EVONNE: No. Thank you. Mr Edwards. I'm fine.
MR EDWARDS: I've booked a practice court at 9 a.m. I want you there at fifteen minutes to. And not a minute later.

MR EDWARDS *exits.* EVONNE *slams a few backhands into the court.*

SCENE 20: THE FRENCH OPEN AND THE BILLABONG DRESS

The court transforms to an ochre red. EVONNE *is hitting out on a French Open clay court. Everything is slower, larger, more pronounced. The* DANCERS *lift* EVONNE *and slide her from side to side. The sound of sneakers sliding on clay, the puff of dust.*

EVONNE: I love playing on clay courts. The slippery red dirt. Just like home. The ball moves slower. Everything moves slower as you slide into play. I know exactly where the ball is going to land, even before it's been hit. I'm in my element.
I took my very first Grand Slam Championship at the French Open in Paris in 1971. I was seeded number three. Not too bad for my first appearance.

EVONNE *is given her trophy and she raises it in the air. The audience cheers. She hands it to* LINDA *who puts it on the shelf in the family's living room.*

By the time I made it to Wimbledon for my second attempt, I was one of the favourites, so Ted Tinling called up. Ted Tinling!

TED TINLING, *a flamboyant English designer, enters with a rack of tennis dresses.*

TED: Darling! Darling! Darling! You are going to *love* this dress! I've designed it especially for you.

EVONNE: Oh, Ted! For me?!

TED *sweeps over to the clothes rack and dramatically reveals a tennis dress from out of its bag.*

TED: The Evonne Goolagong Billabong Dress!

EVONNE: Oh. Gee. Um …

TED: Tall Trees. Still Waters! The media are going to go nuts for this dress! Thank you for inspiring me.

EVONNE: I think it's a bit fancy.

TED: Fancy?!

EVONNE: How about that scalloped one over there with the bolero top?

TED: Evonne! This is your natural habitat.

EVONNE: Ted!

TED: I'll have you know that I have designed for every Wimbledon Champion since 1949. And, Evonne my dear, this year is *your* year.

EVONNE: Well, thanks for your confidence, Ted, but I don't think the world is ready for the Evonne Goolagong Billabong Dress. Besides, the dress code *is* predominately white!

TED: Not this year. This year, I've introduced the colour fuchsia.

EVONNE: You'll get fired!

TED: Let them!

SCENE 21: WINNING WIMBLEDON

Wimbledon Centre Court. The quote 'If you meet with triumph and disaster and treat those two imposters just the same' is projected around the space. EVONNE *and* MARGARET COURT *enter with floral bouquets. They sit and prepare for their game.*

EVONNE: And here I am.
Wimbledon Centre Court!
The Women's Singles Final.
On the Holy Court of the Holy Grounds.
Only this time, I'm ready!

MARGARET *and* EVONNE *step onto the court.* MARGARET *performs her tennis angel serve and volley dance.*

And who's that at the other end? Margaret Court. My childhood idol. I'm nineteen years of age and Margaret is twenty-nine.

The press here in London call Margaret 'Big Marge'. And she is big. Huge! In height and strength. She's won more tournaments than any other lady on the circuit and has the biggest serve in the women's game. There's nothing you can get past her. She can reach everything!

WIMBLEDON OFFICIAL: Time, ladies. Mrs Court to serve.

The game begins and MARGARET *serves a cracker.* EVONNE *hits it back and they dance out a gladiatorial game.* EVONNE *has the upper hand.*

Snap to the Goolagong family lounge room. KENNY, BARBARA *and* LARRY *are glued to the television set. It flickers in the dark.* LINDA *enters with a plate of food.*

LINDA: What did I miss? What did I miss? What just happened?

BARBARA: Mum! She's won the first set!

KENNY: That's my girl!

LARRY: Go, sis! Go, Eve!

LINDA: I can't look! How many more games does she have to play?

LARRY: Depends. If she wins this next set, she wins Wimbledon.

KENNY: That's my girl!

BARBARA: But if she loses this set, it'll go to three.

LINDA: Three whats?

BARBARA and LARRY: [*together*] Sets! Mum!

LINDA: I can't look, I can't look, I can't look … I'll make us a cup of tea!

LINDA *exits to make tea.*

Back at Wimbledon, the PLAYERS *prepare for the second set.*

LARRY: Mum! Quick! She's back on.

LINDA *enters.*

LINDA: I can't look! I can't look! I can't look!

KENNY: That's my girl.

ALL: *Go, Evonne!*

EVONNE *serves an ace.*

EVONNE: I took the first set 6-1 and played even better in the second! It was like a dream! The *Princess Magazine* made real.

EVONNE *and* MARGARET *slug out the final game of the match.*

Backhand.

Forehand. Forehand.

Backhand.

EVONNE *hits her championship-winning stroke.*

And so I guess that's it? I'm the 1971 Wimbledon Women's Champion!

She raises her hands in the air. The audience applaud and cameras flash

EVONNE *shakes* MARGARET*'s hand at the net and* PRINCESS ALEXANDRA *hands* EVONNE *the plate.* EVONNE *holds the plate up high and the press cameras flash.*

The London press found some new nicknames for me that day. They called me …

REPORTER: 'Sunshine Super Girl'!

EVONNE: … and then followed that up with …

REPORTER: 'Babe from the Bush'!

The words 'Sunshine Super Girl' and 'Babe from the Bush' are projected onto the screens. EVONNE *puts her trophy in her bag and puts on a pair of over-the-knee suede boots and takes off her tennis skirt to reveal a little white pant suit. A disco ball and music plays.*

EVONNE: I wore my Ted Tinling mini pant suit and over the knee boots and danced the night away. Even Mr and Mrs Edwards got up and had a dance.

EVONNE *slips away from the party and phones home.*

Hello? Barellan pub?

KENNY *jumps on the phone, puffing and panting.*

KENNY: Evie?!

EVONNE: Dad!

KENNY: You did it, my darling girl!

EVONNE: I won! / I won!

KENNY: / That's my girl!

EVONNE: How's Mum? Where are the kids?

KENNY: We're all here. The whole town's celebrating!

EVONNE: Where's Mr and Mrs Kurtzman?

KENNY: They're here too! Mr Kurtzman says you've gotta do more work on your second serve!

EVONNE: Haha! Tell him I said thanks for the coaching advice!

KENNY: Oh, you looked good on the tele, darling! Hang on. Mum wants to talk!

LINDA: Hello, darling!

EVONNE: Mum!

LINDA: Did you have a lovely day?

EVONNE: Yes, Mum! I had the best day ever.

LINDA: When you coming back home?

EVONNE: Soon.

BARBARA: [*offstage*] Mum! Something's burning on the stove!

LINDA: Hang on!

LINDA *exits.*

KENNY: We're proud of ya, love!

EVONNE: How's that old car of yours going?

KENNY: Ah, she's alright. She's up on the stumps at the moment.

EVONNE: Maybe I can buy you a new car.

KENNY: Ahh. You don't have to do that.

EVONNE: With my winnings! I gotta go! I'm running out of coins! Tell everyone I'll be home soon. Love you!

KENNY: You're a champion, my girl!

EVONNE *hangs up the phone.* JOHN NEWCOMBE, *replete with handlebar moustache, enters and joins* EVONNE. KENNY *puts Evonne's trophy up on the shelf in the family living room.*

EVONNE: The next day, John Newcombe and I are the guests of honour at the Wimbledon Ball. It was another Aussie assault. Thank God Mr Edwards taught me how to waltz! You try doing the three-step to 'Tie Me Kangaroo Down Sport'!

EVONNE *and* NEWCOMBE *dance awkwardly.* EVONNE *puts on a brave face.*

After the ball we went to Knights on Knightsbridge and danced the night away. I even had a celebratory shandie!

EVONNE *returns to her hotel room from the ball alone.*

And then I'm back in my hotel room and my feet are killing me!

She takes off her knee-high boots and turns on her red transistor radio. It plays a melancholy tune.

I haven't seen or heard from Roger all year and he's stopped replying to my letters.

Well, I'm not exactly a conventional girlfriend, am I? I can't even sneeze without it being written about in the media. No wonder he's got cold feet.

Oh well. At least I get to finally go home next week.

SCENE 22: HONORARY WHITE

Back in Australia. EVONNE *is packing her suitcase.*

The words 'Evonne Goolagong versus Aborigines Advancement League' are projected up onto the scoreboard.

ISABEL *and* BOB *from the Foundation of Aboriginal Affairs enter wearing protest T-shirts and headbands.*

EVONNE: Izzy! Bob!

ISABEL: So are you going to play?

EVONNE: I'm just a tennis player.

BOB: While you were busy getting your MBE, us blackfellas were pitching a tent in Canberra.

EVONNE: The Embassy. I know. I saw it on the tele.

ISABEL: Things are really hotting up.

BOB: They bashed the shit out of us.

EVONNE: I know.

ISABEL: The media talk to you! They won't give us the time of day!

EVONNE: I'm not political like you two!

BOB: They listen to you.

EVONNE: What am I gonna say?

BOB: That you won't play until South Africa repeals its racist apartheid laws.

EVONNE: I can't do that!

ISABEL: Why not?

EVONNE: I've got my reasons.

BOB: It's a white supremacist country!

EVONNE: I'm gonna talk with my racquet. This will be the beginning of the end of apartheid. Just you wait and see.

BOB: And betray your people?

EVONNE: I'm not betraying anyone.

ISABEL: That's not what it says in the newspapers.

EVONNE: I don't read the newspapers.

BOB: Listen, Evonne.

He grabs a newspaper out from his back pocket and reads it.

'What she is about to do will never be forgotten. She will not be remembered for her tennis, but as one who sold out responsibility to her race for the prospect of being a white for a week.'

EVONNE: What do they mean, 'white for a week'?

ISABEL: Evonne, the South African government is making you an 'honorary white'.

EVONNE: What?!

BOB: So that you can play in their racist tournament! [*He continues reading the article.*] 'She will never command respect either among her own people or white people.'

EVONNE: Who said that?

ISABEL: Aborigines Advancement League.

BOB: So, are you gonna play?

EVONNE: I dunno … I just …

ISABEL: Will you use their white toilets or the one for the blacks?

BOB: You're a Jacky Jacky!

EVONNE: I've been turned away from two discos. One in Brisbane (you remember Bob) and the other one in Melbourne when they let my white friends in, but wouldn't let me in! *And* I had to sit at the front of the cinema at Condobolin with my brothers and sisters when I was a kid. What difference does it make whether I play here or in South Africa?!

We've only just got the right to vote!

BOB: Yeah, well, choose them …

ISABEL: Or us.

EVONNE: Mum always says, 'You treat everyone the same.' If I play there now, it'll open the door for others like us.

ISABEL: Yeah well, don't forget ya mob back home living under the poverty line.

BOB: Tennis is a whitefellas game anyway.

BOB *and* ISABEL *exit.*

EVONNE *hesitates.*

She closes her suitcase and the court transforms to the South African Open.

EVONNE: The truth be known, the South African tournament was just like any other. Dressing-rooms, practice courts, lunch room, gardens … A perfect world. Or was it?

A BLACK MAID *enters and takes Evonne's suitcase.* EVONNE *steps onto the court and prepares to serve.*

And there they are. The 'whites only' seats. And way over there up the back in the corner, the 'black' seats.

And here I am. This novelty. This apparition. This 'Honorary White'!

She serves an ace. The crowd cheers.

And every time I win a point the biggest noise comes from way over there up in the back in the corner. The 'black' seats.

Every bone in their bodies wants me to win. The white fellas want me to win too. They can feel a change coming. I've never wanted to win so bad.

I only made it to the quarter finals that year.

But when I came back the following year …

She slams an ace down the line.

I beat them.

I won that South African tournament.

The first ever 'black' woman to do so.

A DANCER *hands* EVONNE *her trophy. She raises it in the air towards the 'black' seats. They sing her a traditional African song.* EVONNE *hands the trophy to* LINDA *who puts it on the shelf in the family lounge room.*

SCENE 23: WALKABOUT WITH STRING

EVONNE *looks intently at the strings on her racquet, framing her face as she talks.*

EVONNE: String.

She checks the tautness of the strings on her racquet.

It's a powerful force. String. It holds and binds us together.

The PLAYERS *enter the court and perform a 'women's string-making dance'.* EVONNE *joins in.*

Stringy bark, animal fur, human hair, grass.
It holds and binds us together.
Twine these strands together.
Roll 'em on your legs.
Up and down.
Yarning circle.
The aunties.
The sisters.
Legs red raw.
Little hairs rolled off.
Feels good.
Busy flat hands.
Roll 'em on your legs.
Up and down.
For hours.
For days.
That string.
She strong.
Real strong.
She carries your tools.
Makes nets for the fish and the yabbies.
The giver of life.
String and sinew.
Our protector.

Men chew sinew.
Sticky like glue.
Like the grip on my racquet.
Taut.
Bound with love.
Connecting me to you.
Connecting me to Country.
Of Country.
This string.
I know about you.
This racquet.
That net.
These strings.
This ball.

The PLAYERS *finish their string-making dance.*

A TENNIS UMPIRE *breaks* EVONNE*'s dream.*

UMPIRE: Time, Miss Goolagong. Time.

SCENE 24: LOSING KENNY AND WINNING VIRGINIA SLIMS

EVONNE *is in the dressing-room after a match.*

EVONNE: And then I'm back to America on the Virginia Slims Circuit. 'Virginia Slims cigarettes, for a women's only tennis tournament.' And I've made my way up to the semi finals …

MR EDWARDS *enters.*

EVONNE: Mr Edwards. What's up?
MR EDWARDS: Evie …
EVONNE: What?!
MR EDWARDS: I didn't know how to say this to you last night.
EVONNE: Say what?
MR EDWARDS: I didn't want to upset your play preparation. It's just …
EVONNE: What is it?

Pause.

MR EDWARDS: It's your dad. Sweetheart.

EVONNE: What's wrong?

MR EDWARDS: It's Kenny. He was run over. Left by the side of the road … He's dead. I'm sorry, sweetheart.

Pause.

EVONNE: I wanna call home.

MR EDWARDS: I'm sorry, pet.

EVONNE: I wanna go home. I need to go home.

MR EDWARDS: I know you do.

EVONNE: I can't play.

MR EDWARDS: Evie, this is the Virginia Slims Circuit. You're playing in a team.

EVONNE: I have to go home.

MR EDWARDS: There's nothing you can do for your dad now.

EVONNE: Mr Edwards!

MR EDWARDS: If you go back home now, you may never come back.

EVONNE: I have to go home.

MR EDWARDS: You're one game away from winning the Virginia Slims Tournament.

If you go back home … I'm worried we'll lose you.

EVONNE: I have to see my mum.

MR EDWARDS: I don't think that's a good idea, pet. Just have a think about it, Evie.

MR EDWARDS *exits.* BARBARA *appears in a distant pool of light.* EVONNE *and* BARBARA *are speaking on the phone.*

EVONNE: Hello? Barbara?

BARBARA: Evonne.

Silence.

BARBARA *and* EVONNE *are speechless. Open mouths. A silent wail. Snot and tears.*

EVONNE: I'm coming home.

BARBARA: There's nothing you can do now.

EVONNE: How's Mum?

Silence.

I'll be on the next flight.

BARBARA: You're in the finals! We'll be okay.

EVONNE: It's just tennis! I'm coming home.

BARBARA: You can't let down your team.

EVONNE: I know, but …

BARBARA: Dad would want you to play. Play.

EVONNE *hangs up the phone, picks up a trophy and holds it sadly into the air.*

EVONNE: And so I beat Chris Evert in the final and won the Virginia Slims Championship.

We won that trophy for Kenny Goolagong.

BARBARA *takes the trophy and puts in on the shelf in the family living room.*

I miss his warm brown skin.

The way his hat always tilts to the side.

Car rides on the dusty roads.

Laughter and hugs.

Always warm.

Always.

EVONNE *walks to the opposite end of the court and looks back at her family home.*

I never came back for Dad's funeral.

And Mum never forgave me for that.

No more 'Goolagong Three'.

Just me.

Evonne.

On the other side of the world.

END OF ACT THREE

ACT FOUR

ON HER OWN

SCENE 25: HELL SCHEDULE

MR EDWARDS *enters with a schedule.*

MR EDWARDS: Now if you play at Singapore, play the Federation Cup in Spain and work your way up through Europe and Canada you'll be in good form for the US Open. This is *your* year to win that US Open.

EVONNE: [*looking at the schedule*] But there's only two weeks off for the whole year!

MR EDWARDS: You won't win the US Open taking holidays!

EVONNE: I want to go and see Mum.

MR EDWARDS: You can go home in December.

EVONNE: That's four months away!

MR EDWARDS: You can have a break before the Aussie Open. See ya family then.

EVONNE: Can't I just skip the Federation Cup?

MR EDWARDS: And not play for your country?

EVONNE: I haven't seen Mum since Dad died.

MR EDWARDS: We'll get you home in December. *And* you'll have a US Open trophy in your hands.

EVONNE: If we skip the Spanish tournaments I can get an extra two weeks with Mum *and* still have the US Open trophy.

MR EDWARDS: You sure about that?

EVONNE: Yes! I'm sure!

Pause.

MR EDWARDS: Alright, pet.

EVONNE: Yes!

MR EDWARDS: But you'll still play the Federation Cup?

EVONNE: Thanks, Mr Edwards.

SCENE 26: MR EDWARDS INSULTS EVONNE AT THE BAR

EVONNE *plays like her life depends on it. Like, if she wins this game, she'll get to go home ...*

EVONNE: Backhand.
Forehand. Forehand.
Backhand.

She stops playing. She's exhausted.

I play that hell schedule and collapse in a heap in Canada with a chest infection! I pull out of the tournament and am laid up in my hotel room for days, when suddenly …

There is a knock at the door.

ROGER: Gong?
EVONNE: Roger?

ROGER *enters.*

What are you doing here?!
ROGER: I heard about your dad. I'm sorry, Evonne.
EVONNE: It's okay.
ROGER: About everything. I didn't want to distract you or get in the way of your career. You were the favourite at Wimbledon, for godsake!
EVONNE: Oh, it's good to see you!
ROGER: Come on, let's get you better …

He helps her to a seat.

EVONNE: We hole ourselves up in my hotel room, make a little nest, and Roger nurses me back to health. We're like a pair of teenagers. Gee, it's good to see him.

ROGER *exits.*

When I finally get myself to the US Open I only make it to the first round. Lost to an American player, Pam Teagarden.

The words 'Aussie champ goes walkabout' are projected around the space.

I dunno. I just can't get my mojo out here today.

MR EDWARDS *enters. He's drunk.*

MR EDWARDS: Oh! There she is! You played like a bloody C-grade player today! You're away with the bloody fairies! Haven't got your eye on the ball, have you? Well, we all know why you've taken your eye off the ball, don't we?! Too busy running around with what's-his-name!

No winners' waltz for you this year! Go on! Go back home! Go and ring what's-his-name.

EVONNE: I'll see you in the morning, Mr Edwards.

MR EDWARDS: Gutless! Bloody gutless!

Do you want to be a tennis player or a housewife?!

MR EDWARDS *exits.*

SCENE 27: MARRIAGE AND DIVORCE

EVONNE: Well, I did go home and ring 'what's-his-name' and I arrange for Roger to fly to Pittsburgh to meet me.

ROGER *enters and holds hands with* EVONNE. *They face each other.*

Roger and I get married in London at a registry. We duck in between tournaments to avoid the media. I wear a plum-red dress, chuck a flower in my hair and that's it. I promise Mum we'll have a church wedding in Barellan. But for now, I'm on the circuit.

ROGER *puts a ring on her finger and they kiss.*

When Mr Edwards criticises me in the press for losing Wimbledon because of a 'honeymoon hangover' it's clear to everyone that my coaching days with Mr Edwards have come to an end.

EVONNE *and* MR EDWARDS *are facing each other. She hands him a letter. He reads it.*

MR EDWARDS: Is that what you want, Evonne?

EVONNE: Yes, Mr Edwards.

He folds the note.

MR EDWARDS: I see.

Pause.

EVONNE: I appreciate everything that you and your family have given me.

MR EDWARDS: You won't win another Wimbledon with a baby on your hip!

You've ruined your career!

EVONNE: We'll see about that!

MR EDWARDS: You're on your own now!

MR EDWARDS *exits.*

SCENE 28: ROGER AND ME AND BABY MAKES THREE

EVONNE *practises tennis, like her life depends on it.*

EVONNE: He was so wrong.

It's 'love all', all round. And I don't mean 'zero'. I mean big fat-hearted love. Roger and me …

Pause.

… and baby makes three.

She stuffs a towel up her top.

The media said I couldn't do it too. That having a baby would set me back.

She trains on the court whilst pregnant.

Well, it didn't. I keep training and training. Right up till I'm seven months pregnant.

ROGER *enters.*

ROGER: For goodness sake! Do you want to have this baby on the court?

EVONNE: Well no. Not, really …

ROGER *leads* EVONNE *off the court. She takes the towel out from under her top and holds it like a baby.*

And when my little Kelly comes into this world, it's like I've won the Grand Slam ten times over. Me and my man. And baby makes three. We're the centre spread in the *Woman's Day*.

'Evonne's Dream Home' and a happy snap of EVONNE, ROGER *and baby Kelly are projected onto the screens.*

The *Woman's Day*! Mum *loves* the *Woman's Day*!

EVONNE *is back up on the court.*

And then we're back on the court.

Backhand.

Forehand. Forehand.

Backhand.

Roger and I are juggling child-minding duties and training. I'm up all night feeding and down on the court during the day. And I bounce back alright. I've gotten myself back up into US Open contention. Finally! I'm in the semis with Martina Navratilova.

MARTINA NAVRATILOVA *enters and serves to* EVONNE.

Backhand.

Forehand. Forehand.

Backhand.

Ahhhhhh!

EVONNE *holds her calf muscle in agony.*

I hear the snap. Martina hears it too. She keeps serving and playing wide. Making me run from this side of the court to the next.

EVONNE *struggles to reach the ball.*

Backhand …

Forehand …

Forehand …

Backhand …

Forehand …

Forehand …

EVONNE *breaks down. She limps to her chair.* ROGER *leaps over the fence to her side.*

ROGER: Are you right, Gong?!

EVONNE: Roger, you're not supposed to be on the court!

ROGER: Come on.

EVONNE: I'm right!

ROGER: Let's get you in the dressing-room.

EVONNE: No. I wanna play.

ROGER: Evonne, you can't.
EVONNE: They've come to watch me play.
ROGER: It's not worth it!
EVONNE: I can do it!

She gets back up on the court and serves.

I play the rest of the match. It's an ugly game. But I have to finish it. I just have to.

EVONNE *shakes* MARTINA*'s hand at the net. The headlines 'Mrs Cawley crashes!' and, ironically, 'The best loser of them all' are projected around the space.*

SCENE 29: WIMBLEDON COMEBACK

ROGER *is strapping* EVONNE*'s ankle.*

EVONNE: My legs just aren't the same after I had Kelly. It takes months of injections and treatment to get my fitness back, but I get my rankings up and I make my way back into Wimbledon contention.

EVONNE *changes into a Fila tennis outfit.*

The BBC say I'm 'not a factor'. But when I beat Betty Stove in the quarter finals the London press have a field day with my 'housewife status'.

The headline 'Mrs Cawley mops up!' is projected around the court.

REPORTER: Mrs Cawley mops up!
EVONNE: Oh, is that what I do out on the court? A bit of housework!
When it comes time for me to face Chris Evert-Lloyd in the finals and attempt a Wimbledon victory after nine years (with husband and baby in tow!) I feel strangely calm …

The court glows a luminescent green. EVONNE *prepares for the match of her life.*

It's a cloudy day. The air hangs like a big black blanket. Flashes of sunlight, taunting us.
My mouth is dry.
Everything at Wimbledon is timed to precision.

Like a gold Rolex watch.

Roger looks nervous.

UMPIRE: Mrs Evert-Lloyd to serve.

EVONNE: Chris serves and we smash away at each other at the baseline.

It's a long rally. Chris attempts a drop shot and it loops miserably into the net.

The crowd groans.

Chris's timing is all over the shop and I capitalise on that.

I take the first set 6-1.

UMPIRE: New balls please.

EVONNE: Roger does a quick nod. Encouraging.

The clouds loom.

I win the first game of the second set and we swap ends, only to be rudely interrupted by the star of Wimbledon …

The rain!

Back to the dressing-rooms, and after sixty-three minutes, the rain finally stops stealing our thunder!

But the damage has already been done.

Like a true champion, Chris has gotten herself together in the dressing-rooms.

UMPIRE: Mrs Cawley to serve.

EVONNE: I bounce the ball with determination and smash it. Chris hits it back a beauty.

We boom away at the baseline.

Change of ends. Take a seat. Towel on face. Wipe hands dry. Quick look to Roger, but not too long.

Pensive.

It's four games to three and Mrs Evert-Lloyd is in the lead.

No time for prissy-ness now! Track that ball like a snake! A quick backhand volley and back to the base. Chris has determination in her eyes. And before I know it, its five-all and Chris has got three break points.

I save the first one with my famed backhand volley—but dammit, she comes back and breaks my serve!

UMPIRE: 6-5. Mrs Cawley to serve.

EVONNE: Change of ends. Towel. Drink. Settle. Break her serve. Break it. Push her to a tie-break.

Please don't let this be a three-setter.

With every ounce of will in my body, I channel the spirit of god-knows-what and I break Chris's serve.

This match will be decided by a tie-breaker.

There's not a peep in the house. You could hear a pin drop.

It's my serve—a quick rally and Chris hits it out. Unforced. And I'm serving in the tie-break, five-three.

Chris attempts a tricky drop shot and it blows a raspberry in her face—dropping shy of the net and taking the Centre Court crowd into contortions.

Chris to serve. I crouch. Prepare. I've got three Championship points.

The Centre Court crowd smell victory. They want a third set!

But I've got other plans.

Chris serves and I hit it back too hard, it goes out.

Damn …

Roger bows his head. Has he actually stopped breathing?

I've got two Championship points. Mine for the taking.

UMPIRE: Quiet please. Quiet please, ladies and gentlemen.

EVONNE: Chris serves. Backhand, forehand, backhand, forehand. One, two, three hits over the net—a quick rally—and then *bam*!

I've won!

The crowd cheers and screams. People are on their feet. Jumping up and down. Cameras are flashing!

Did I just do that? Win Wimbledon? Again?!

Roger's mate pats him on the back.

Curtsy. Hold that golden plate and raise it in the air!

ROGER: That's my girl!

EVONNE: That year, the London press have a new name for me.

They call me …

ALL: 'Super Mum'!

The words 'Super Mum' are projected around the space.

EVONNE: And yes, I had a 'lovely day'.

Thank you, Mum.

And then I'm thinking about Barellan.

Mr and Mrs Kurtzman. Mr Dunlop who leant me his racquet. The butcher's daughter who gave me her tennis shoes.

My mum Linda. Dad Kenny. Barbara and Larry. Dot and Clarrie Irvin. Mr Dicker at the petrol station and even Mr Edwards.

EVONNE *puts her trophy on Kenny's shelf in the Goolagong lounge room.*

The DANCERS *and* ACTORS *watch her and address the audience.*

DANCER ONE: Evonne Goolagong Cawley has won ninety-two singles titles.

EVONNE: Did I win that many?!

ACTOR TWO: Fifty doubles

EVONNE: I never used to count.

ACTOR THREE: And seven majors.

DANCER TWO: Two Wimbledons.

DANCER ONE: One French

ACTOR TWO: And four Australians.

DANCER TWO: She was the first 'black' woman to win the South African Open.

DANCER ONE: The *Open* that was *closed* to many.

ACTOR TWO: She's been number one in the world and travelled far and wide.

And then …

EVONNE: I came home.

Back to Australia.

EVONNE *steps up onto the umpire's chair and throws a fishing line into the river.*

The other day I was shopping at our local supermarket and I'm waiting in line at the checkout, when I can feel this woman staring at me and staring at me. I looked away, and then back again, and she was *still* staring at me. This happens sometimes, but anyway, finally this woman plucked up enough courage and came up to me and she said …

DANCER TWO: Excuse me, but did you used to work at Coles?

EVONNE *chuckles to herself. A fish bites.*

EVONNE: Hey, look out! I've got a bite! Yeeeee!

She reels in the line.

Why me?

Why not?

The sounds of a tennis game and commentary become louder and louder. The audience cheers.

Lights slowly fade.

THE END

From left: Luke Carroll, Jax Compton, Katina Olsen and Kyle Shilling in the Performing Lines/Griffith Regional Theatre 2020 production. (Photo by Jamie James)